STRAY HARBOR

poems by

Rage Hezekiah

Finishing Line Press
Georgetown, Kentucky

STRAY HARBOR

Publisher: Leah Maines

Editor: Christen Kincaid

Cover Art: KT Morse

Author Photo: Sarah W. Newman

Cover Design: Jessica Yurkofsky

Printed in the USA on acid-free paper.
Order online: www.finishinglinepress.com
              also available on amazon.com

Author inquiries and mail orders:
Finishing Line Press
P. O. Box 1626
Georgetown, Kentucky 40324
U. S. A.

Table of Contents

I. COVE

II. BAY

To Rosetoes

I. COVE

TEMPERANCE

At six, I craved the crash of glass,
my want electric and unslakable,

for the shattering sound like a fissure.
Familiar. My mother broke dishes, drunk

with rage, flung ceramic onto the cement
from our back porch. Her laughter

punishing the silence of no one to blame. I'd wait
and pitch her abandoned bottles, wet and lipsticked,

onto the pavement. I stood above a broken meadow
awaiting fresh wreckage. Dad cracked walls,

hurled furniture, whatever nouns his hands found.
He pulled my bedroom door clean off its hinges,

to find me cowering behind a vacant frame.
In my parents' final fight, they emerged

from the basement streaked with ancient
paint, wearing evidence of an explosion. Both

marked our hardwood floor with ghostly
footprints, a subtle tutorial in animus.

KITCHEN CHILDREN

My father mourns the sweet work of his black daddy's hands,
my grandfather's island accent swaying names, *boy* and *child*.

Poppy's kitchen simmered, stove and oven steaming
with coconut bread and jerk chicken.

His slippers whispering down a single hall
toward a cascade of seed in backyard birdfeeders.

Then, wetting the moss beneath the bonsai on windowsills—
a gentle attention to growing tiny things.

My father mourns the soft, pink palms of this man's hands,
who gifted him reticence and welts from belted leather.

He only remembers waterfall sounds
of seed poured in the feeder, piquant curry smells,

how many times he lay the spoon
in sweet repose between the burners. Not how he raised

the spoon to remind them: love is earned
by staying small and quiet. Like birds. Like bonsai.

MY FIRST JOB

Eight years old,
in a well-worn soccer uniform,
I wrapped an empty coffee can
with bright paper, stood outside

the corner store, asking for donations.
Kind neighbors, unknowing,
poked folded bills through
the top-slot I had cut

in diaphanous plastic.
Opening my cow eyes wide,
I'd flash an innocent smile,
feel the power of persuasion.

Later in my bedroom, I'd count
the dollars, arrange change
in tiny, powerful towers,
tuck it all into the envelope

taped beneath my underwear drawer.
My hustling uncle taught me
this trick, inspired my careful hiding.
Deception, a tool honed

and wielded proudly, the reward
for an unsupervised child.

SALEM

At nine I understand the solitude
of the cove before dawn, and steal
across the street while my parents sleep
facing opposite directions. They won't know
the way I strip bare on this beach
to swim in darkness. Only when my feet
can't find the bottom do I fear the ocean,
and yet I bargain, dare myself
to swim where I can barely touch. If I reach
the buoys, they'll be no more yelling.
The check won't bounce at the grocery store.
Mom's car won't hit the median
when she comes home from the bar.
My fingers barely brush the bobbing mass,
but any contact counts. I rush to shore,
stand on land, wrap myself in a plush bath towel
so big it drags along the sand.
At home I've learned to push my clothes
against the edges of my bedroom closet,
when I do, there's space enough to sit.

MY FATHER, SWIMMING

Waist deep in ocean, he was not my father.
Laughter spilling loudly from an open mouth,
his wetblack skin gleaming unfamiliar.
The hands that I had come to fear
acquiesced in seawater. I watched him
anticipate the splash of each wave
as though amazed.

He'd never been a child,
those shrouded years,
as the sole black altar boy at Dorr Memorial,
the one dark child on the diamond
of Walter Flynn Field. Watermelon forbidden
by his father, eaten in secret. Reticence
was commanded, austerity is the father I know.
How could it have been him, swimming?

But my father was volcanic, his eruptions capricious.
He'd have me retrieve his leather belt
before bending me over his knee.
In the water, I saw him surrender fierceness,
his large palms drawing circles around himself.

BLUEBERRY PICKING

We choose the ones that seem to pulse
heavy-ripe from hours in full sun,
stretch the fabric of t-shirts taut—
a hammock for collection. Bellies full
of fried scallops, ice cream,

constellations of fresh freckles on our faces.
We know nothing of loss.
Vaguely keeping watch, our aunts
and uncles park in lawn chairs on the porch,
filling glasses with fresh ice, tonic and gin,

overpriced limes from out of town.
We're not allowed to swim to the dock alone,
we need life jackets and bums on seats
when we take out the canoe. Lily's last summer
she'd just turned ten, Aunt Nessa let her

paint her nails bright pink at the lake.
The grown-ups remain hushed
and focused, like they're trying to remember
stage directions. Last time we saw fireworks,
I said they made me think of Lily,

mom's eyes met mine sharp and silent.
Only once I tried to ask what happened—
she studied the horizon. *We move forward.*
It's the only direction God gave us.

ON HEARING THUNDER

My barefoot mother dares the cove
to liberate its storm, raves from our porch.
Worn from years of childrearing, she

welcomes capricious sky, beckons
the scent of asphalt-ocean. I am a vessel
brimming with uncertainty, cautious

in the constant shifting of my adolescent body.
Called to her side, I feign belonging
as she bellows into grey air, a sorceress

hoarding orbs between her palms. Together
we await the gale's arrival, thick drops pummel
the steps as we climb, moving deeper

into heavy rain. We open windows, allow
our wooden floors to swell. A storm door woman
with no glass left, I'm in her wake becoming her replica.

SEEING MY FATHER'S PENIS

My father stood, and the black horn of himself slipped

    through the fly of his boxers in our Floridian hotel room.

        Flaccid, it looked like a mistake, gathered and external—

accidental. He was oblivious, walking between the queen beds,

    while my sister and I sat giggling in Disney pajamas. This part

        was not what I expected, dark skin folded under vulnerable skin

at the apex of his legs. At eight my mind conjured a pink cartoon,

    the relic of an animated film I borrowed from my local library.

        The white women kept my card stored

in a small plastic box behind the children's desk. I loved watching

    their manicured hands, flicking through the cardstock dividers,

        fetching something only mine. The laminated card I'd signed

with amateur skill, birthed a new freedom, my young mind teeming

    with too many questions. I was ravenous for answers like a wolf pup

        seeking carrion. In the room with my father, I had too long to inspect

his body, understood him knowing would mean shame. Rosie and I hid

    under quilted covers, wordless and quaking with nervous laughter.

        We took turns peeking out from beneath our homemade fort,

            confirming it was still there

                hanging in the air,

                    an apology.

FEBRUARY COVE

We are ten and bundled crown to toe
scaling frozen boulders on the beach,
our parents home and snow day drinking
no longer watching from the window.
I claw wet rocks in your wake, desperate
to keep pace, soak my wool mittens through,
neglecting numb hands. You are a boy
fresh with adventurous, outdoor ideas,
brimming with strange stories. As we climb
you tell of sharp-toothed creatures buried deep
in frozen ocean, point into the distance
where jagged rocks break the placid ice,
a hundred little births along the surface.
With our arms spread wide we run
along the snow-covered sand, almost expecting
to be caught, like how we secretly hope
we're found during every game of hide and seek.
Bathed in a frantic energy we generate for fun,
both of us panting plumes of warm breath
into air, salted-cold. We embrace the tension
of fear and exhilaration here,
the last great year of our imagination.

LEAVING THE TAMARACKS

We didn't sense the cadence of vacation's
ending, our wet bathing suits pressed
against the station wagon's leather backseat.

Giggling, unaware, my sister and I let damp hair
leave slug-like streaks behind our heads,
feeling no dread in the premonition

of September. Calluses on our feet
from a summer outside, our soles toughened,
a natural protection. Far from home, we forgot

how warm months shielded us
from harm. We only knew
the long drive meant ice cream. *I want*

black raspberry with rainbow sprinkles
in a sugar cone. Rosie always gets chocolate.
Over-sunned and dosed with sweets, we slept,

our bodies buttressed together in sticky, sated calm.
Four small palms cradled beach stones,
seashells, detritus all worth saving.

PHLEBOTOMY

My inner elbow acquiesces the pin-prick,
surrenders in the latexed palm

of a stranger. Moat gates lift, reveal
familiar piping—veins resembling my mother's,

that climbed her wrinkled hand like branches.
I used to sit beside her on the couch, and press

my fingertips into tributaries beneath her skin's vellum.
I'd observe the resilience plumping the tubes,

giving way to delicate pressure. Today, claret color
fills the vials, I give, knowing it was never mine.

LAYERS

After Seamus Heaney

All the lemons lit in the kitchen bowl
seem softened by the sun, whose morning lull

illuminates your hands splayed
open on butcher block table.

Oh, what you can make with your hands,
and how I ache to witness

your wooden spoon mixing six
simple ingredients in a ceramic vessel.

Bake me a cake again. Place squash blossoms
and nasturtium on the plate,

spread the pastry with sweet cream,
a meditative motion, slow and serene.

Mamma, once you made such gentle things.

OUR FIRST PIE

Emma visits bearing apples,
a bushel from her Maine orchard,

and during her stay we bake our first pie.
I stand at the sink, running water over

ripe fruit in the colander, and she pulls
cutting boards from the cabinets. We drink

mulled cider as we slice, collecting cores
in a bowl for compost. In my mother's kitchen

we sing and giggle, wiping our hands
on checkered aprons. She tells stories

about farm life: the lambing season last spring,
the blight that killed the heirloom tomatoes,

her plan for ridding the greenhouse
of hornworms. Dusting the rolling pin

with flour, we take turns leaning into the dough,
forming two circles for top and bottom crusts.

The house smells of cinnamon when we sit
cross-legged by the hearth, until the timer dings.

My mother comes home, and finds us proud
and pleased, celebrating our creation.

Standing in the doorway with her coat still on,
she frowns, *What do you think, you invented pie?*

FOR ROSALIE

You lean in, click-snap your compact open,
and dab the sponge in foundation.

Silent, and skilled with a fluid motion
your arm extends, you softly press

nutmeg-colored cream, our shared complexion,
onto my chest and neck. From the back

of our mother's car, you spare me
her wrath, covering fresh marks

from the lips and teeth of my first girlfriend.
Your touch sororal, you apply concealer,

knowing the difference
between shame and discretion.

ADVICE

Marriage is like shoveling shit
against the tide, she says,
toasting no one. I nod, placating
my drunk mother, to sustain her calm.

Donna comes through the back door,
another bottle of Chardonnay in her fist,
her long skirt smelling of patchouli. They howl
and cackle, grabbing glasses from the cabinet.

Her arrival means I'm free, but these familiar women
have me spellbound, I'm only ten,
listening as they fail to censor themselves.
Men? Who needs 'em?
What a fuckin' waste of everything.

After the divorce, my mother
paints our home pink, deems it
The Feminist Safe House. Still,
years later, she's panicked and upset
when I've fallen in love
with a woman.

KEEPING UP APPEARANCES

In the tradition of stiff drinks
and troughs of white wine

we've been trained to deny,
to remain in the realm of *I am fine.*

I unlearn the familiar *good good good*
of our Caribbean grandfather, and forget

how to answer *how are you?* Practice
saying *well*, focus on my health—

I tell you I'll do anything,
in part to dismantle the guilt

of leaving you too long
with a drowning mother.

She's offered vague apologies before,
for things she won't remember

that we can't forget. In sobriety
she believes a single trip to confessional

where she tells of her abortion
absolves it all. We're the ones she kept.

I wear a three hundred dollar dress
at your wedding, shoes and jewels

that match the sea breeze swatch
you've carried in your clutch for months.

You coordinated every decoration
with desperate precision, an effort

to control something tangible.
Twenty years ago, at family events

we kids tried to hide the cassette tape,
attempted to prevent the part

where all the adults cut loose
to that B-52's album. Our mother

and her brothers, ruddy and sweating,
clothes specked with the wet of spilled rum.

Puddles on the hardwood. What if we tried
to stop them because it made us unbearably sad?

FOR MY MOTHER

Bloated on the beach, a rotting seal carcass
claimed the shore, the morning

of your other daughter's wedding.
We paused our screaming at each other

to shoo the dog away from angry flesh,
open as a horn. We'd come to watch the sunrise, after

you cradled me in the spare bedroom
sky still dark, legs bare beneath the sheets—

your mammalian form warm and familiar.
In a time I can't remember, I slept against your chest,

fed hard at your breast, my full lips firm against
umber areolas. At dawn, our women bodies

intertwined in a twin bed imbued safety,
we held each other, sleepy skin on skin.

My mother, with the intimacy of a lover
both of us vulnerable and swaddled in flannel

I forgot not to trust you. We freed ourselves
from heavy down, pulled on sweatpants,

sweaters smelling of wet wool, you
wrapped an imperfect scarf around my neck

that you knit your first year sober. We drove
through the vacant town, past birch tree boles

lining the Morse code of road to Crane's Beach,
the vast marsh swathed in bleak horizon. I tried

to tell you something true, but denial is our family
tradition, the legacy of Irish-Catholic guilt. I wanted

to call the dog back towards the seal's corpse,
beckon him to drive his snout into the carrion,

force you to witness a mess so awful
not even you can deny it.

YUCATÁN

I traded one black dog for another
        my mother says, of the Rottweiler

she brought home from the shelter
        after she'd peppered our front steps

with my father's clothes. She
        was drinking & he'd cheated,

so we got a puppy, a round
        bundle with a bark like a bird. Three

women & a dog, living
        in *The Feminist Safe House*—

her name for the cove home
        she reclaimed, painted the soft pink

of rose quartz. My sister & I
        danced to the Indigo Girls while

mom taught us misogyny—
        men as enemy. We traveled

to Isla Mujeres, feasted on fresh
        fish & papaya for breakfast, swam

in a local cenote. Liberated,
        we climbed Chichén Itzá's 91 steps,

flexed our biceps at the apex,
        chanting *sisterhood is powerful*

at mom's command. She snapped
        photos to bring back, all of us

freckled, sated. On the return flight,
	nestled in the middle seat, our mother

kissed our sun-bleached curls, saying:
	We don't need men for anything. Not a damn thing.

II. BAY

TINCTURES

My two fingers trace
your deepest part, your béchamel,
flick half-smoked cigarettes
in the bedside bowl.

This our topography,
the differential abuse of our bodies—
your father with his flame,
my father with his leather.

Cotton straps cover minefields,
salve for our weary
tendons, our flesh rubbed,
whetted mouths upon our wounds.

BARN SHOES

I scrub my brick red clogs clean of caked sugar
when I leave the bakery. Barn-dancing in the kitchen,
I wrap sweet butter with parchment,
mark the floor with flour beneath my feet.

Ruth wore shoes like these in Salem, drove north
to her horses' stables, while homesteading in the city.
She allowed her lamb to roam behind her house,
found it drowned in the backyard meditation pool.

Calm in the loss, she offered me clement weather,
even when I pummeled her daughter in a snowdrift.
My fists cold and wild beneath barren grapevines, a madness
only six years old can know— still Ruth spoke softly,

I see how angry you are, just come inside. Her hands warm
on my chilled earlobes. Within her arms' broad cradle,
I heard the woodstove crackling, and cellared chickens
roosting in sawdust, finding home in their own down.

HUNGER

I was waiting for a body unmine
to do the womanly work of swelling,
spilling open. I yearned to bleed
& burst, to render myself round,
curve into a circle. I feel the flesh

of my own form now, press
my palms against my breasts
as though I have earned them,
grown them from seed. My desire
will not shy, this source will nourish

another. But the mantra of your touch
reminds me: *Make love of yourself perfect*,
as though this is enough. If I was given
this gift, let me suckle somebody
who needs me, let me feed the living.

BOTANY

Roots reach deeper in distress,
penetrate and grasp humus—
I envision the elephant roots

of the copper beech, each pendula's branch,
an arc of heavy hearted arms.
In stress, trees touch new depth,

re-commit to standing firm.
Grounding down, they resolve to stay.
I am not this way. I am deciduous.

I find that I love her and want to flee.
Leaving is familiar. Surrender,
my seasonal affliction.

But she leads me by the hand,
words like salve, I don't mean
to believe her, but I do.

I practice standing still, forming new growth
above and beneath fertile ground. If I grow
anything, it will be in spite of myself.

FULL BELLY FARM

We pile into the Datsun's bed, beneath
the morning California sun. Bouncing
over farm terrain towards the field,
all of us wield freshly sharpened knives.

Thick red and green stripes
of cabbage ribbon the distance.
Knees bent, we begin the collection,
hurling heavy vegetables into bins. The men

are always laughing, a sexual joke
in every action. They hunch
behind each other, feigning penetration.
I'm always laughing too. We pile the boxes high,

pausing to swig water from delicate plastic cups.
Pancho asks, *Raquel, te gustan hombres o mujeres?*
Qué piensas? My reply a question. *What do you think?*
Then he pulls a worm from dark soil, a thick form

wriggling in his fingers, *Cómalo, Raquel! Eat it!*
I tug the writhing thing from him, open wide
as the other men freeze in disbelief. The form bursts
between my teeth as I chew, grainy and bitter,

and I refuse to flinch. Proving I belong
among them, I'm strong enough to stay.

FIREFLY

You were aglow, sharpening yourself
against the lake-night sky. In a wooded cabin,

lit by milky harvest moon, I lay awake.
Traces of city life surrendered when you arrived,

luminous, hovering above the bed. But you
froze before me, caught in wisps invisible,

your wings' resistant vibrato in her web.
I turned toward the dull buzz of you,

saw your flickered light hum among the cricket din,
your body dimming, a brief autumnal hymn.

NESTS

As a girl I searched for harmed birds,
broken creatures to contain
in straw-filled boxes. Determined

to find a tiny, mangled body,
I'd approach slow, arms wide, seeking
something barely breathing.

Hard-wired for exigence, desperate
to protect. Now, smitten with the crisis
of a love who hates her own reflection,

my obsession won't rest. Let me fix you.
When you say you need me, successive ee's
spread your brittle teeth wide,

withstanding so much self-abuse—
a diet of mint gum, fizzy water, hard candy,
food that will not feed you. I'm powerless

in your resurrection, you're not a starling
anticipating hands to hold you,
set you gently in a make-shift nest.

Those I thought I'd saved
were not awaiting rescue, they were only
making their own way home.

OFF THE COAST

I fished with my father, who fished with his,
both of us learning to plunge
hooks into writhing night crawlers,
in hopes of luring trout and bass,

scaled, silvery things for dinner.
I never shied from eating their crisped skin,
blackened by the grill. It all seemed natural,
a slice of New England living.

I'd planned for a certain kind of harm,
sitting on the catamaran's edge, I watched
the waves trail behind us, ready. My filament
of fishing line angled from a heavy pole.

Why, then was I terrified snagging a bird
who'd flown too close? I cringed seeing it
flap and flail, wings beating the ocean's surface.
Only willing to kill a single kind of creature,

featherless, with vacant eyes, far removed
from human. The crew cut the engine,
set the brown booby free, unfamiliar men
in life vests, desperate to stop my screaming.

PLAYING FETCH

You pull the ball from the jowls of our dog,
his tightened teeth clenched against
a round, familiar form. *Let it go*, you say,

I understand his resistance. Hind claws
piercing the mud in the dooryard, his hinged jaw
determined to keep what he's earned.

Your pas de deux, a proximal tug of war
is a mirror, the relentless grip of his maxilla
and mandible, fixed on baring down.

Life asks me to release my grasp, to trust,
and I remain unwilling. Even daily meditation
won't relieve my fear— I'm trained to fight.

Knowing you won't win this, I stand beside you,
rest my face on your shoulder, my palm pressed
at the small of your back. *Just let him have it,*

I say, and watch your hand bloom open.
At the corner of the orchard, he holds
the ragged orb firm between two paws, regal

holding court. He gnaws the prize
he's won, satisfied. Who are we
to teach him any different?

POINT REYES

We board the excavated toy
beached boat wide as a whale,
while dark birds perch port
& starboard. Riskless in our twenties
free from the stranger of worry, we trespass
fearless of tetanus threat—
accroach the abandoned vessel,
its hull launched in sand dune mouth
of marram grass, a hulking mass—
ribs with no heart. We expose
ourselves to its slick sides' perpetual rust,
man-made form smothered
in cultivated barnacles, history's
detritus. In awe at the helm
we hold hands & touch
each surface, greedily tactile
did you see this? Look—
I want to believe age
won't surrender adventure
that my life can still be so palpable,
cloaked in electric moss
I run my fingers over.

DOZEN

Winter holds the light close,
tight against its chest,
before dawn warms
wet hay beneath our feet.

Frost clings to each blade of grass—
what little growth remains before snowfall.
We unearth the flannel and down,
smelling of cedar beams.

I watch her calloused hands
in motion, a fragile strength easing
into each nesting box
where laying hens await

her tender reach. I think: *Yes.*
I would wait quietly too,
my eyes closed knowing
she would come every morning;

the grasp of her hand
below my body's down,
retrieving what I'd made
while she was sleeping.

PSILOCYBIN

You and I ride our bikes to Ipswich River
and I dispense the only advice
I've been given. *Just let them take you,* I say,
placing a small handful of caps in your palm.
We sit on the muddy shore eating tuna,
anticipating magic. A slow undulation sets in,
its pulse warming the wet ground, and we lie
watching trees become hands holding everything
to the sky. I can smell my own sweat
and I'm weeping about my attempts to mask this scent.
You're crying too, about how you hate your cunt
and I'm telling you *Your everything is beautiful.*
We watch a shallow puddle teem with the life
of tiny organisms. Pressing our arms into the mess,
we roll around and giggle. For hours we swim and sing,
until we mount our bikes again, stopping at a farm stand
to fondle the summer berries. Lambs bound about
their pastures and I watch your face collapse
as you realize they're food, the awful truth
of cycles. The meadow's full of alyssum
and clover, the August breeze sweet.
I want it all for as long as it will last.

A GIRL & HER DOG

The dead dog is a bag hanging
from the arms of a frantic girl,

hands full of an animal
she loves. After collecting his body

she carries him with no direction—
paces a jagged circle, from house to car,

an effort to rescue what's already gone.
Twin mammilla, milkless, mark the pale fruit

of the dog's belly, his hind paws
pendulum-swing.

You & I sit close on the bleachers
across the street in earshot

licking ice cream cones as the sun
sinks below the treeline, surrendering

a pink July sky. It isn't right
to be so separate from the loss

we don't mean to witness
but we don't leave

right away. We hold hands & stay,
wordless, until we can't stay anymore.

LIFE SCIENCE

I plucked an owl pellet from the ground
cradling it, delicate, as if a palm-sized bird

and not the mass of bones and fur purged
from a second stomach. In science class

as a girl, I learned these dark forms teemed
with the remnants of undigested pieces.

Wielding a small scalpel, my latexed hands
unfolded the debris, bits of spiny tail,

shards of teeth and claws. Sharpness cased
in what looked like hardened mud, but wasn't.

I was fascinated picking it apart, plunging tweezers
into particles of animals long dead. The girl beside me

raised her palm, tentative into the room's warm air,
but they don't look like they could hurt anything,

eyes fixed on color photos of their feathered bodies.
We'd been told owls eat their prey whole.

I'll never know, I thought, *who's capable of what.*

III. SOUND

NUDE BEACH

With the rare freedom of being bare,
clutching home-brewed beers in our fists,

we perch on sun-warmed rocks in California.
Queer and stoned, our canvas bags heavy

with farm stand carrots, local peanut butter,
seeded bread from the nearby bakery dumpster—

provisions for sunset. Our unshaven legs lined up
like variegated piano keys, we roll thick joints,

raise a kite into the sky, release the line
'til it ascends beyond the thin stripes of cirrus clouds.

From our backs, we watch it soar for hours, staking
our claim to this small patch of sand, a haven

for three bodies on a handmade blanket.
Nobody can say we aren't women,

our breasts splayed, dark hair blooming
between our legs, beneath our arms. Unashamed

we smell of earthen smoke. Like a team
of harbor seals, we sprawl across each other,

bark and giggle, until the watermelon sky
hugs the Pacific. Here, we lay down our longing.

An unexpected coven, we reclaim the bellow
of our voices, revel in our natural power.

MIRABELLA POOL

Her infant body bobs below
the chlorinated surface,

over and over she goes under,
screams and chokes each time

her mouth opens into air—
A primal howl ricochets

off cement walls, trapped
in echo. At the child's side

an adult in a wetsuit
marked *Instructor* stands

in shallow water, submerges her
and waits for the babe's face

to reappear saying *Yes, Good Job, Gaby,
Good.* I can't look away.

After each lap of breaststroke
I return to stare, pretend

to adjust my goggles
watch her not drown,

near drown, on a loop
that won't relent. She's learning

not to swim, but to self-rescue,
roll onto her back to float,

find breath and repose.
But these are foreign lessons,

she can't understand or consent,

only panics for her next breath

while her parents stand by, detached.
This is for her own good, and theirs,

they come to spare themselves
an accidental loss. First

you teach the child
what it is to drown

so she'll know
to save herself.

BROOKLYN

Under indeterminate sky, rudderless
we lie on a city rooftop and fuck each other
unconscious. Not sorry about our volume,
our unwashed skin, we're stoned, irreverent,
unafraid of consequence. Tomorrow
you leave for California. As you sleep
I watch you breathe, the see-saw
of our shared respiration, my inhale
your exhale, breath's metronome. Before
departure we wash our laundry
in the shower, fill the tub with ripped jeans
smelling of patchouli and cedar, a dose
of Dr. Bronner's soap. We agitate
suds with our feet as though we're stomping
grapes into wine. Tell me we'll always be
this young, that you're my cure. We can stay
dazed, directionless, refusing what we have,
what we've been given, reluctant
to take anything by the reigns.

NIGHT SWIMMING

Untethered from bed, you creep towards cool water,
summoned to the community pool.

July's humid night sticking to your sheets,
you duck through an unlocked window,

trace hallway walls in darkness
where floral chlorine blooms.

Your bare feet press against
honeycombed yards of rubber mat,

guide you toward the diving board.
From the thin plank you anticipate weightlessness,

smelling chemicals, entranced,
your focus honed on floating—

you didn't see the bright caution tape
decorating the perimeter, or signs saying *Closed.*

They find you open as an egg,
with nothing aqueous to hold you.

EMPIRE BEAUTY SCHOOL

Students drape black aprons around the napes
of women, mostly women, who squint
at their own reflections. I turn
the pages of *Good Housekeeping*
for something achievable, anything
worth replicating. A layer cake
or feng shui floorplan—
a bento box for what my life could be.
I came here wanting
someone else to wash my hair.

I barely need a trim, but return
knowing the languid motions learning
requires. At the deep sink,
I become malleable, allow her hands
to renovate my scalp. I let her lather
and rinse my curls with warm water.
Seven dollars means contact,
and I don't care what my hair looks like,
I just need to be touched.

FIXING HER TRUCK

Leaning over the complicated interior
of an intricate machine, her white t-shirt

reveals stealth biceps. She reaches
past the carburetor, connecting

a tightly fitted hose, grease between her fingers.
Practicing reiki on the well-oiled wounds

of her Valiant, I am watching, wondering,
what else she can do with those strong hands.

IN THE WALK-IN

You come
from behind—
press me up
against
industrial shelves
fingers tacky
with sugar
my arms full
thick bricks
of butter
tumble when
you kiss
my neck
I tug
your cotton
apron's edges
waist strings
bow loose
at your back
undone
I wrap your fists
in bondage
pull you
closer
taste your
salty neck
a gloaming
redolent
meyer lemons
heirloom tomatoes
fresh sage
I'm holding
your face
in my hands

ANDROGYNY

You were the last man inside me.
Now my girlfriend and I snip the balls
from the purple dildo I won

at a feminist raffle, and trash
the pink-skinned dick
which slipped into her harness—

reminding me of you. I tried
to learn to let you fuck me,
but lusted after every

punk-girl bassist at basement shows,
whose hair obscured the features
of her face. I allowed desire

in darkness, telling myself she *could be*
a boy. Watching her, riveted,
angular blond bangs hung

like a scrim, bright eyes beneath—
I learned want. Her fingers firm
against the neck and fretboard

of her Fender, head bowed
in reverence to her own
powerful hands, summoning song.

SEEING YOU ON FACEBOOK

You've created
what you longed for
all along
you &
a heroin addict's
ex-girlfriend
calling any place
home
the way knitting
is only
pulling loops
through rows
of loops
your recipe
for desire
so blatant
a haven
you've come to
wanting
I wanted
to give it to you
when we were
nineteen
you
were in recovery
from your rape
& I learned
rape happens
when anyone pretends
not to hear no
women
can do this too
I guarded
you
like a warrior
but wished
it didn't influence

our lackluster
sex life
I'm selfish
I wonder how
you got this girl
to fuck you
remember
how
after our first time
you left the room
& retched
I stood outside
the bathroom door
listening to you
empty your insides
choke & empty
pause & empty
I pretended
this didn't
turn me on
I shouldn't
be jealous
now I see
how a family
means belonging
you found
a home
a woman
to call you hers
I never wanted
you that way
& yet
there's something
about resentment
what I've chosen
separate from regret
a thing surrendered

but part of me
still wishes
you were not okay
I should have
been the one
to make you whole

HONING

Sprawled open, my v-wide thighs
held the faucet hostage
awaiting the eruption I'd found
while filling myself,
bringing water deep
into my own brimmed vessel
beneath lips vast enough
to hold a fist, no—
a body newly mine
I gave myself to this, a bath
and time alone to bloom,
submerged in bubbles
my budded nipples piercing
the steam-filled room. Tight
breath muffled under
thunderous rushing, the water—
thrummed relentless
in the best way until
I spilled over, sinking
bicuspids into my bicep
blossoming/breaking
into affirmation: *yes this*
a new kind of wholeness
both/and
yes

LEARNING ABOUT BOYS

You held it,
flaccid in one hand,

strangely proud of your body.
You've never rubbed one out?

As cousins we'd learned
each other's anatomy, asking

questions, showing and telling
in bedrooms, while our mothers

cackled in the kitchen, over glasses of Shiraz.
I was unready to understand

this part, but you stood beside me
and I couldn't keep myself

from looking as you began to tug
and shake, your eyes closed

and your face in awe of something
I couldn't place. When you came,

a thick stripe of fluid hit the futon, sounding
like a small bird falling from a nest.

AT THE ARTISTS COLONY

A loon's melancholy call
alights the lake, lonesome
as a plum at rest in an open

palm. These women,
poised with artistic prowess
ever angled toward the light

do not want approval,
they've been taught
to shrug off affirmation,

dismiss kind words
about their work,
do not try

to tell them otherwise.
We've all been trained
to avoid vanity, listen

with receptive attention,
already sorry for
what we've made, or said—

our strange bodies lush
with surreptitious lust
for people we can't *really* fuck.

We've been warned:
do not be a teacher's pet,
a sycophant, perfectionistic,

a prude, do not be
a goody two-shoes,
a loud-mouthed slut.

Apology is female,

a concession. Nobody
asks the men

about children,
only what they've come
to produce. Praise

as welcome as an egg,
they know they're good,
and aren't afraid

to hold the space of yes.
Doubtless, they don't cry
when someone says

you're here for a reason.
You belong. They know—
they were born knowing.

AUTUMN

Everything is brighter before it dies—
the sugar maples blood-shock red,
like the last haunting of November. We
offer up soggy paper bags
pregnant with detritus:
hydrangea effigies, necrotic roses
autumn's decomposition ready
for surrender. I feel this loss in my body,
the emergence of bleak days I can't control
when the trauma rises under my skin
blackening my light. The trembling fear
of the beaten child returns, vocal chords
hoarse from begging, and then
the resolute detachment. In dramatic reenactments,
men who worked the fields only cried out
after the first two lashes, and then their skin—
open as a fish, the red flesh raw. They went absent
as an elephant, left their bodies and their masters—
Is this skill implicit in blackness? Did my father
do this too? Hand his mother the leather,
disappear behind the dark lids
of his own eyes, not looking,
seeing nothing.

MY MOTHER ROLLS US A JOINT WHEN SHE VISITS ME IN CALIFORNIA

In poor light, bent over a squat kitchen table,
she lifts a rolling paper from the pack,
pinches it between thumb and pointer, slow
like a magician preparing to impress. I watch
the bright shine of her salmon manicure
crease the bottom fold, a gulley
for the substance. She removes a sticky clump
of medicinal grade bud from a wide mouth mason jar,
applies light pressure, sprinkling tiny pieces
across the furrow's surface, like when
she sows the garden with alyssum and clover
each spring. Moving with acute precision, she twists
the ends of the delicate splif closed,
lifts the gift toward freshly lipsticked lips
and runs her tongue along the paper's crisp edge.
Kissing the tips of her fingers, she blesses
what she's made us, reverent
toward the holiness in her own hands.

OUR BIKE TRIP

Some farmers we met invited us to their wedding,
halfway through Washington state. Like sisters,
we pulled borrowed dresses over our heads, paisley
and cotton, revealing feral underarms. We bartended drunk
in an open field beneath Cassiopeia, passed a full flask
of bourbon between us behind the bar—
Barefoot we ran through black woods to drag the keg
from creek, waded too deep, soaking our skirts,
reckless and wet. At night's end we found men to kiss—
I grabbed an older teacher with a full head of curls
and led him behind the red barn, ran my fingers
through his ringlets and wished he was a woman. While you
found a boy barely of age and brought him back
to our shared bedroom. Men are so simple
we didn't know we could have been kissing each other.

Notes

"Blueberry Picking" borrows a line from the film, *Wish I Was Here.*

"Layers" is after Seamus Heaney's *Mossbawn: Two Poems in Dedication.*

"Hunger" borrows a line from Nisargadatta Maharaj, offered in a meditation led by Tara Brach.

"Mirabella Pool" is based on the Infant Swimming Resource's Self Rescue program, which trains infants in the survival technique of rolling onto their backs to float and avoid drowning.

"Empire Beauty School" and "For Rosalie" were co-translated into Spanish with Sol Colmenares Rodríguez for publication in the journal *Juana Ficción* in Cali, Columbia.

"Fixing Her Truck" was inspired by Lizi Brown's painting entitled Slant Six #64.

Acknowledgements

Sincere gratitude to the following publications where many of these poems first appeared, at times in slightly different versions:

Amethyst Arsenic, The Aurorean, Baltimore Review, Banshee, Blue Lyra Review, Caesura, The Cape Rock, The Carolina Quarterly, Chicago Quarterly Review, Columbia Poetry Review, Diode, Fifth Wednesday Journal, Fjords, Freshwater, Glassworks, Hayden's Ferry Review, Juanna Ficción, the minnesota review, Mom Egg Review, Mosaics: Independent Women's Journal, Mud Season Review, Natural Bridge, Nepantla, Off the Coast, Painted Bride Quarterly, Plainsongs, Poetry East, The Portland Review, Rattle, Really System, Riding Light Review, Salamander, The Shallow Ends, Tampa Review, West Branch, Zone 3.

Thanks also to the following anthologies, for publishing and/or reprinting these poems: *All We Can Hold: A Collection of Poetry on Motherhood*: "Layers," "Our First Pie," *Nasty Women Poets: An Unapologetic Anthology of Subversive Verse*: "Full Belly Farm," *Ungatherable Things: A Word Portland Anthology*: "Mirabella Pool," "Honing," "Our Bike Trip."

Finishing Line Press, thank you for believing in this book and ushering it into the world.

Also thank you to Lisa Mangini of Paper Nautilus Press for selecting my chapbook, *Unslakable*, as a 2018 Vella Chapbook Award Winner.

To Cornelius Eady and Toi Derricotte, thank you for Cave Canem, and showing me that I belong. To Cave Canem faculty and fellows, thank you for inviting me into the fold and pushing me to grow. I'm honored to be among you. Special thanks to Brionne Janae, Clint Smith, and Amber-Flora Thomas for blessing me with your words and championing my work.

Thank you to the MacDowell Colony, The Ragdale Foundation, and the Saint Botolph Foundation for the blessing of quiet space.

Gratitude to Sara Siegel and the Mass Poetry Foundation for continuing to give poetry a voice in Massachusetts, and making me part of the community.

Thanks also to Terrance Hayes and the Hurston-Wright Foundation for seeing promise in my early work.

John Robinson, thank you for seeing me as a writer, and showing me the way.

John Skoyles, Jabari Asim, Gail Mazur, for your patience, honesty, and persistence, thank you.

Thank you to my community, for holding my hand, reminding me to breathe, and cheering me on: Natasha Cecere, Sue Harvey, Lisa Winner, Laura Campagna, John Allen Taylor, and so many others.

To my family, I'm so blessed to be loved by you. Thank you.

Mom and Dad, watching you devote yourselves to art and music helped me believe that I could do this work. You taught me not to settle, thank you, I love you.

Rosetoes, our laughter is medicine, may it continue to heal us.

To Lou, you hold the space every day. You fill me with light, I'm so grateful for your tenderness.

Finally, thank you, reader for holding these words in your hands.

Bio

Rage Hezekiah is a New England based poet and educator, who earned her MFA from Emerson College. She has received fellowships from Cave Canem, The MacDowell Colony, and The Ragdale Foundation, and is a recipient of the Saint Botolph Foundation's Emerging Artists Award. Her chapbook *Unslakable* (Paper Nautilus Press) is a 2018 Vella Chapbook Award Winner. Rage's poems have appeared in *The Academy of American Poets Poem-a-Day, Rattle, Salamander,* and several other journals and anthologies. You can find more of her work at ragehezekiah.com.